Praise for *I Tell You This Now*

When I read Daniel Lawless's poetry, I feel as if I am in the presence of an understated visionary. Deeply personal, his poems move on two levels— they are both in the world and looking down at it, as from above. They are poems of the ordinary and of a soul seeking redemption. They are poems of memory and suffering, longing as well as of celebration, insight and blessing. I am in awe of this poet and of this ingenious and luminous collection, *I Tell You This Now*.
—Nin Andrews

The essential humanity of Daniel Lawless' voice hall marks *I Tell You This Now*. The poems are narrative yet complemented by an imaginative filtering of the actual world, supported by an exceptional eye and ear for the plaintive detail of the past. These poems are honest, credible, and compelling as they excavate the light of meaning each poem reaches for and grasps. I love the idiosyncrasy combined with clarity, and how what is often a surprise, (a linguistic prize) in the line or paratactic leap is absolutely necessary to the thought, soul, and emotional center of the poem. This is authentic, expansive, and conceptually balanced at once—a remarkable lyric depth and appreciation of our lives.
—Christopher Buckley

The poems in Daniel Lawless' *I Tell You This Now* evoke the photos of Diane Arbus in that they might make you want to turn away, but then only to turn back and go deeper, as he does, to find the humanity in this complex, difficult world. He mines photographs both real and imagined to create fresh, startling insights that sustain us, like the small daily joys of "…lumbering the cha-cha as she boiled the green out of Thursday cabbage." The collection unspools in one long, magnificent section—nothing to slow down or stop the accumulating momentum of these brilliant flashes. They're like old flashbulbs that briefly blind us as they sear into our consciousness. Death and illness hover over this book, as they hover in our lives, even as we hurtle ourselves forward. As Lawless writes, "how the dead live on/These scraps of memory we feed them like dogs./Always hungry, come-calling us by their name."

There's a brilliant darkness to these poems that are full of light.
—**Jim Daniels**

Daniel Lawless' *I Tell You This Now* is an exceptional book--a book of unflinching, immense candor and excruciating irony. "Your dead father who is beautiful like *Quang Duc setting himself aflame*/You'll announce to the night-nurse, vaporous with morphine." It is, as well, a book of elegies in which the standard modes of presiding over bereavement do not apply. The book is haunted. The dead walk. And they die in sanitariums, soiled hospital beds, and iron lungs, and in poems of wildly unwinding page-long sentences of extraordinary vigor and figuration. *I Tell You This Now* is a completely engrossing and disquieting work. I recommend it wholeheartedly. I am gratified to have read it.
—**Lynn Emanuel**

Daniel Lawless' extraordinary new book *I Tell You This Now* dazzles with poetry's strange power—"negative capability"—the courage to be vulnerable even in the moment of insight, to work at the threshold where the self ends and the street begins, to be the animal that knows it will die. It's an anarchic power that subverts all authority, including the speaker's. Adamant in their modesty, generosity, and ferocity, these poems can critique the absolutes–the giving of names ("Daniel"), the arc of time ("Sleek Green Car"), emptiness itself ("Ullage"). Always these poems speak to the real, the loved, the broken. Always the work is haunted by the injustices we suffer and inflict in a world which is collapsing inwards–"your dead father who is beautiful like Quang Duc setting himself aflame." Lawless' poems are wild, but search for a way to be responsible in a time of chaos. They live on the breath, but they bear the charge of a lifetime. Lawless is a visionary, a craftsman, and a terrific poet.
—**D. Nurkse**

"The slight trembling of words on white pages opened on a table/Like the trembling of grass or water deep in the wells," Daniel Lawless writes in a poem from his astounding new collection, *I Tell You This Now*. Haunted by adolescent cruelties, sexual abuse, family illness, suicide—these poems speak of seemingly unspeakable personal matters as they retrace steps to

invoke the dead or emotionally scarred whose intense presence nudge us back to the starting gates of childhood where life's trajectories can be rewritten: "How marvelous/it all must have be turned into a ghoul with your friends to yearn and yet not to know yet/what that yearning meant." Long-lined constructs of sensory imagery and highly charged language carry you into a world where even language itself trembles. *I Tell You This Now* disarms with bold candor and a disquieting clarity.
—**Dzvinia Orlowsky**

In joy and terror all at once, the shining elegies and buoyant love poems of *I Tell You This Now* by Daniel Lawless unfold. Lawless has the uncanny ability to create piercing elegies that behave like tender breakup poems. His love poems are no less sublime. (After minutely describing a farmer's vintage tools, he dissolves them to lingerie… The result is a love poem that ends both very far yet very close indeed to those historical implements.) One of the deep pleasures of reading *I Tell You This Now* is that you never know quite where you're going until you get there. And getting there means getting it: the shock of gorgeous and gruesome recognition in each upturned world in Daniel Lawless's remarkable poems.
—**Molly Peacock**

We write the poems we have to write. Thank God Daniel Lawless had to write the poems in *I Tell You This Now*. Out of compulsion, beauty. Out of pain, humanity. Out of memory, a hard-won sense of proportion. Out of love and fear and horror, the sometimes perverse pleasures of achieved art. In his poem "Why Write," after a particularly disturbing narrative of parental abuse, Lawless finishes this way: ". . . if I could carve / a poem out of this I could do anything?" Not write anything, do anything. This book is about survival—emotional, existential.

"The opposite of play is not work, it's depression," says Stuart Brown, of the National Institute for Play. And Lawless knows this, never forgetting to do what poets must do: romp with language— strike one sound against another for the sheer joy of it, balance on the beam of syntax, fling metaphors like skipping rocks on a lake. As Robert Frost so memorably said, "Only where love and need are one, / And the work is play for mortal stakes, / Is the deed ever really done…)

—Ron Smith

The vital subject of Daniel Lawless's latest book, *I Tell You This Now*, is the "once" of childhood as he suggests in the poem of that title—a gone but still going world that exists forever in the liminal space between "wonder' and "wince." One lives there as a "ghost inside another ghost / Un-pierceable by anything in the substantial world." And yet pierced the reader is, and deeply, by these hauntingly elegiac poems, each by turns heartbreaking and humorous, allusive and probing, scary and pleasurable, devotional and transgressive, as they and the poet seek nothing less than to rescue the dead who "live on / These scraps of memory we fed them like dogs"— the dead who uncannily desire to rescue us in our afterlife of losing them.
—Daniel Tobin

I Tell You This Now

Daniel Lawless

Červená Barva Press
Somerville, Massachusetts

Copyright © 2024 by Daniel Lawless

All rights reserved. No part of this book may be reproduced in any manner without written consent except for the quotation of short passages used inside of an article, criticism, or review.

Červená Barva Press
P.O. Box 440357
W. Somerville, MA 02144-3222

www.cervenabarvapress.com

Bookstore: www.thelostbookshelf.com

Cover Art: Barn, Lake George (1936) by Alfred Stieglitz. Original from The Art Institute of Chicago. Digitally enhanced by raw pixel. Canonical URL https://creativecommons.org/publicdomain/zero/1.0/

Cover Design: William J. Kelle

ISBN: 978-1-950063-80-2

Library of Congress Control Number: 2024931817

ACKNOWLEDGMENTS

Grateful acknowledgement is made to the editors of the following journals in which a number of these poems originally appeared, a few in slightly revised versions:

2 Horatio: "On the Way to Your Funeral, Already Sleep-Deprived"
Asheville Review: "From the Afterlife"
American Journal of Poetry: "Pigeon-Toe," "Home Visit," "On Her Death Day," The Kingdom of the Ill," "Sonnet for Tony," "When I Got the News," "It was there," "Why Write?," "Crazy Lady"
Barrow Street: "Ullage"
Copper Nickle: "Childhood"
Dodge: "Prayer"
Dreaming Awake: New Prose Poetry From the US, UK, and Australia: "In S—," "1.8.20" (The Visitation), "Revelation on Pearson Avenue"
JAMA (Journal of the American Medical Association): "Sleek Green Car"
Los Angeles Review: "Daniel," "[I tell you this, Tom, because you are dead]"
Manhattan Review: "Phyllis Pleasant, 14, A "Sweet" Surprise,' "Anonymous Girl, Aged 17, "Cured" Awaits Her Departure from St. Anthony's Hospital," "Once"
Marsh Hawk Review: "Aglet"
Massachusetts Review: "5.23. 20"
New American Writing: "Not Fireflies," "The Paten"
Ploughshares: "Freundenshreck"
Poetry International: "My Brother, Solar Eclipse, 1965"
SALT: "Milady, She'd Say"
SOLSTICE: "Poem Against the Rich"
Unbroken: "The Uncanny"
upstreet: "Dither," "Boyhood," "The Mask," "In Basel," "Aster," "Elegy for the Dying Pit Bull," "Ars Poetica," "Etched Pewter Bird"

To my parents, my brothers and my sister, a few friends and their ghosts who linger among the dictionaries and sanitariums.

TABLE OF CONTENTS

Family Photograph: My Brother, Solar Eclipse, 1965	3
Boyhood	4
Freudenschreck	5
From the Afterlife	6
The Paten	7
Not *Fireflies*	8
Aglet	9
Coincidence: A Love Poem	10
Etched Pewter Bird	11
Milady, She'd Say	12
On the Way to Your Funeral, Already Sleep-Deprived	13
Once	14
Elegy for the Dying Pit Bull	15
5.23. 20 —	16
Since Yau Died, M —, *Untethered*	17
The Kingdom of the Ill	18
Ullage	19
Sonnet for Tony	20
The Mask	21
Rose	22
The Arts of Love	24
Scraps	25
Pigeon-Toe	26
In S—	27
"Dora S —, 8, Home Unit Iron Lung"	28
"Phyllis Pleasant, 14, A "Sweet" Surprise"	29
"Anonymous Girl, Aged 17, "Cured" Awaits Her Departure from St. Anthony's Hospital"	30
"Tommy S—, 11, Local Socialite's Son, After His First 'Field Trip' to Bardstown, Kentucky,"	31
"Nurse S —, the Florence Nightingale of the Polio Ward"	32
Aster	33
Sleek Green Car	34
I Tell You This Now	35
Poem Against the Rich	36
Revelation on Pearson Avenue	37
Home Visit	38
1.8.20 —	40

The Golden Frog	41
Crazy Lady	42
Whoopee!	43
Ear Plugs	44
Why Write?	45
Prayer	46
In Basel	47
When I Got the News	48
Lonely Marriage	49
The Uncanny	50
Daniel	51
Dither	52
It was there	53
Ars Poetica	54
Childhood	55

ABOUT THE AUTHOR

I Tell You This Now

"We all have an old knot in the heart we wish to untie."
—**Michael Ondaatje**

Family Photographs: My Brother, Solar Eclipse, 1965

In a year, Haldol, ECT, the closed gates of a sanitarium.
But for now—how happy you were.
To be eleven and unconcerned
For once with school, the Cubs, who punched who.
For a few minutes to be unlearned, to be taught
A new world. O, distant boy, how marvelous
It all must have been, to be turned into a ghoul with your friends,
To spurn the murmur of grown-ups with their highballs and hair
On the deck for a lowering sky burned sepia, orange.
At three o'clock to feel yourself disappear inside yourself —
To cast no shadow. And—so long ago now
how did you put it?—the delicious, insistent thought
What if it stays like this? To yearn and yet not to know yet
What that yearning meant.

Boyhood

And now we come to the poem of the great mystery
Of the years 1957 - 1963. As you can see,

It's a short poem, with just enough room
For the apple core I broke my front tooth on,

One of Mary Kay Johnson's pigtails, an invisible photograph
Of my brother waving though the iron gates of a sanitarium.

A King Edward Cigar box of a poem, let's say, where,
Emptied of its jackknife, centimes and wax lips, a parakeet

Might face eternity serenely nestled in a wad of Kleenex.
Or maybe even a shed-sized poem, the dank, mysterious

One with jars of rusted nails and coiled hoses
Behind the garden,

Where I liked to pretend I was flying
Down a long Swiss mountain road on my father's

Flat-tired Schwinn
Propped between two ancient suitcases.

Yes, that's the ticket. A shed-sized poem—nails, hoses,
My dad's cobwebbed bicycle. And I,

Whistling though a missing incisor, ringing
Somewhere in the Alpine air of the years 1957-1963

The bright silver bell of its title.

Freudenschreck

Freudenschreck, or "intense pleasure-fright" —
Leave it to the Germans
To coin a word for the fleeting sense of being seized
By such an inexplicable joy it verges on terror.
Or maybe it's inexplicable terror pretending to be joy.
Also, a physical phenomenon: neurologists say the amygdala
Glows red as a jack ball whether subjects gaze at images
Of planetesimals or gallows.
Picture a joyride, the Appalachian pin-brides of Eugene Meatyard.
Put yourself in the shoes of Aiyana Clemmons, 44,
Of Peru, Indiana, a long-time congregant of the End Days
Christian Church according to the Gazette,
Who may have had a seizure
That caused her to "shiver all over", although another passerby
Reported hearing her shout "Praise Him!" or "Praise God!"
Before "she sort of rocked him"
Before casting that beautiful child into that cold river.

From the Afterlife

My last days were not so bad, my ex-wife says from the afterlife,
Not so bad as you think. So relax.
The Home Helpers you hired didn't steal from me
As far as I knew, neither money or my Dilaudid—
Or have their boyfriends over as if I were blind *and* deaf.
I especially liked the Dominican one,
Alaia—Lord, the stories she could tell!
I read, watched a lot of television, if you can believe it,
Baseball, if you can believe it, Maddow, the food shows.
You remind me a little of Bourdain. Sexy, but no beast. Seriously,
Though –*Chilaquiles*! *Tariflette*! I don't think I weighed
Ninety pounds. Can you imagine? White as a ghost.
But here's the thing. Happy, Daniel. You can't imagine.
What did Thoreau say? *I grew like corn in the night.*
On the inside. Well, there was only the inside, really,
I was flying inside myself, like Bill Knott. It was dark,
But I wasn't scared. I made my own light. A bioflurescent jellyfish,
Like at Monterrey. Other times, I sprouted legs.
Long, beautiful legs with glitter-spritzed toenails like Alaia's.
I remember visiting her mother's orchard,
I was the highest lechosa on the tree no one could reach.
What do the French say? The *disparition de* _____?
When I woke up, I had disappeared.
My old grass hut/ lived in now by another generation/
Is decked out with dolls, wrote Basho.
Does that help, Daniel? Or, remember that trip to Lucerne?
Imagine it went on forever. Not so bad.
I, watching you watch me write my name
In fogged breath on a windowpane
And watching it disappear.
Stepping outside some inn or other
After the thunderclouds rolled past,
Everything calm, reticent. How like the Swiss
We could see the Alps everywhere
From wherever we were standing.

The Paten
— from Holy Instruments

Imagine a lidless Silent Butler, or somebody's grandmother's fancy candy dish—this polished bronze plate with a rich mahogany handle "employed to catch the tiniest precious crumbs of the Body of Christ," according to *Learning to Serve.* Below, the scuffed marble communion rail. Above, long rows of mouths gaped, candlelight struck their gold fillings. O, parched tongues! O, Clearasil and ear wax, quivering chin hairs! Sometimes, for a joke, you jabbed your friends in the neck with it, friends that are dead now. And once, in the dim sacristy, vain Father R—, regarding his graying beard in the paten like a mirror; then in the rectory twice more, moaning as he caressed my nape...

Not *Fireflies*

In the South, but plainer:
Lightning bugs.
Not as the poets would have it, *you dears*
Carrying your little lanterns behind you,
Green stars, or the faulty strike of a match;
Not as you once imagined
The visiting souls of your dead parents.
Only you, poor boy, lonely god
Of the backyard,
And these flickering insects
Trapped in a juice glass,
To be smeared between your fingers
Or, tapped with a stick,
Set free with a magician's flourish,
According to your cold your wonderous heart.

Aglet

A blood-letting tool, a vestigial claw.
A liturgical vestment, a kind of stitch or stenographical notation,
A vase, a fresh-born eel.
It's fun now to imagine it could be any of these, but
In 1967 the right answer was "the little sheath
At the end of a shoelace" —
Da's nightly vocabulary quiz, home from the Clifton cab-yard,
The summer before for Sean and I would try for posh Saint Tim's.
Years ago now, but I can still see it: his pressed shirt
And flocked cap, that pipe
He claimed the mayor himself had given him.
The two of us watching a drop of spittle trickle
The length of its lacquered stem as he continued
"...from the Old French, aiguille, "needle,"
To point or pierce. Colloquially a small sorrow.' "

Coincidence: A Love Poem

Let's face it, it had been another one of those days.
I can still see us: I with my Sunday macchiato, my balding head
as usual buried in the real estate section of *Le Monde*,
you with your hot chocolate and extra sweater
cross-stitching yet another blankie
for somebody's grandson Jake,
as we sat as usual in companionable silence
on our regular afternoon bench outside Sheltam's, each of us it
seemed trying not to remember it was our 32nd anniversary.
.
        But, Love, it was just then,

as I was trying to decide this time for good between
un charmant pied-à-terre
dans le quartier animé du 18ème
or perhaps *un cosy «appartement vigneron»*
près de Montpellier historique
…anyway, exactly then that you put down your knitting
and smiled and handed me the muffin
from Levain's you'd saved in your purse all morning,
carefully wrapped in foil under a sturdy paper towel
and wound tight with two twist-ties, but still so fragrant
with cardamom, sweet Carolina ginger, and wild cloudberries.

Etched Pewter Bird

You who are empty and so neither desire
The expensive organic seed mix or require the attentions

Of the fastidious vet, who do not *cheep*
So psychotically cheerfully that sometimes I want to throttle you.

You who do not retreat coyly
From my outstretched hand, or tremble wildly

If I hold you; who never once perched spitefully in the branches
Of the thorny locust tree behind the garage

After I left your cage door ajar in summer,
Or in other seasons mockingly eluded my ridiculous broom.

You, who fix your aventurine eye indifferently upon me
At all times, unlike real birds who if they regard me at all

Regard me suspiciously, or skeptically, and keep their distance,
As if they are tourists guarding their passports.

You, in other words, little generic etched pewter bird on my desk,
Who should signify nothing at all to me, in fact,

Except from across the country the news arrived
Not eight hours ago yet this windless December night

That my oldest friend in this world is dead,
And there isn't anything she or I can do about that.

And my heart, oh my stunned heart, on its cupola of ribs is cold
Now as your weathervane double,

Nameless, hollow, not hawk or sparrow.

Milady, She'd Say,

Ma's liquored-up catch-all address
to her every imagined American better.
One day a Four Roses la-te-da mocking *feckin' Gale Storm
in that sweater* on Dinah Shore, another a poison dart
Aimed at her big-shot employer Mr. Phillips' new Texas bride Bea,
Yee-hawing a jelly-glass gin pretend martini
And lumbering the cha-cha as she boiled the green
Out of Thursday cabbage. Mostly I'd just stare.
And then she'd sort-of cry and distant *sweety*
And you get the picture. This was in the late Fifties
When recent Irish immigrant domestics like her
Must've already been tangled up in their lives,
Their haplessness and fearsome Catholic shame.
Ma's wasn't the only one either.
Sometimes in daydreams I still hear them: *Milady* from
Huge Delia bellowed at a blonde majorette, addled Maggie's spat
At a red-faced WAC as all the downtown maids
Traipsed along a VE Day parade
Through Louisville's Central Park, pissed on pursed bottles of
Cheap Classic Club.
Call it jealousy or a class thing if you want, but that night,
Ma said, she slept better than she had in years. Breakfast,
Late, Lucky's and tea. Da at the pins. *Milady* later still as I passed
By the parlor, snarled once to the dust-specked mirror
Before she sort-of curtsied,
Before I just stared at her packing up before she left us for good
For Galway by nightfall.

On the Way to Your Funeral, Already Sleep-Deprived

On the slow overnight train from Chicago to Altoona,
After people had settled down, having hoisted their heavy bags
Onto the overhead rack and unfurled a magazine
Or unwrapped a tired muffin
Or iffy-looking chicken salad sandwich,
I heard somewhere a few rows up a kid swear, *No,
It was a real-live corpse!* Pretty funny, but

An image that stayed with me all the way to Toledo
As I gazed at my haggard face through the window
In the growing dark, where cows and trees and STOP signs
And here and there an unmoored trailer floated
By as if a dim river had overrun its banks,
As if I were already thinking of them in the afterlife;

Or in a more Zen or theoretical physicist sense
As if, when I let my brow fall against the cold glass,
My own face disappearing, the cows and trees
And STOP signs and occasional double-wide had become
My thoughts alone, disembodied, drifting out
From the Ohio countryside into the vast, unknowable universe.

An image that, inevitably, vanished,
As despite the grinding of the heavy wheels and the screeching
Of the air brakes, I took a little nap, then got up to massage
My aching thighs and use the bathroom.
Which is pretty much where I'd like to leave you, Robert.
Opening the thin little door with a majestic yawn to find
Everyone silently gathering their things

In the half-lit car, the kids rubbing their eyes,
As you wipe your hands on a crisp white handkerchief.
As the porter with his gleaming silver cart
Comes rattling down the aisle
With his fresh *Times* for sale and his steaming croissants,
The tiny bubbles of Perrier rising in their tinkling green bottles
As the voice on the loudspeaker announces *Altoona!
Next Stop, Altoona!* as if it were heaven itself, your own hometown.

Once

Beautiful, gliding word, although perhaps less a word
than an exhalation; circa 1300
a simple adverbial generative—an f-like s become ce
affixed to the Middle English æne, meaning
"formerly, at one time" per the OED. Nevertheless,
its intent always complex, contextual: sometimes a little wince
in there, a little ache. Desire, too. And wonder.
Once, we begin, our lips puckered, as if for a kiss,
but a kiss that never comes, breathless, forever in the past.

Elegy for the Dying Pit Bull

shivering, bloody, curled up against the chain link fence outside
the End Days Christian Church
on 22nd Street: trash and the word MIRACLES in flaking glitter
letters on a strip of plywood
nailed to a catalpa tree. March, maybe April. I remember
an old woman in a flowered
housecoat, Batman mask, a couple of kids in muscle shirts
standing around—one tossed a bite of his candy apple,
not the part sprinkled with nuts.
Maybe the dog started to rise, wagged its tail, a little; sunlight
touched its gold collar, it was as if…but, no.

No, I think that's the whole poem

5.23. 20 —

In the Memory Care Rec Room it's Wednesday,
which means my mother has been 64 Washable Crayola-ing again
the same child's coloring book picture she loves, titled
"Mary Ann and Her New Pal," which is pretty much as you'd
imagine it, except below her as usual
in big block letters Mary Ann is Janice!!!
her dead sister in Galway filled head to toe with Hot Magenta,
and her pal the Peaceful Tangerine horse
whose slightly upturned squiggle
of a mouth she's offering a plump Cerulean apple to
is her faithful husband Bob!!!

Which is pretty much as you'd imagine it,
terribly sad, demeaning, a nightmare
with that vampirish fluorescent lighting, the catheters and oxygen
tanks, and those infantilizing bibs. But
also, I think, maybe a little sweet? Because despite everything —
which is a lot — wouldn't it be nice to see things her way
for once—*dyschronometrically* the head nurse calls it—
a flamboyant kid-simple world
endlessly repeating itself like this? To address
a long-departed sister so joyously,
to take an orange horse for a husband
with such a contented smile as if just then he couldn't think
to want any miraculous thing else
but this beautiful blue present?

Since You Died, M—, *Untethered,*

Maybe, is the metaphor
I'm looking for, as in the bright orange leather

Ball swaying on the pole today in the park before
Some big kid smacked it too hard and sent it sailing

Into the parking lot; or maybe
The thin rope it hung from, frayed at the end.

Or maybe unhinged, not crazy, but think of a door,
The one the hurricane kicked in, how it never swung right after.

I'm talking grief, M—. Great rumbling Red Square tanks of it.
Or maybe think of the grosbeaks

Gorging on the last of the black-striped sunflower seeds at your
Beloved feeder. The black fluster of wings

Before the hard crack before the getting at the soft meat beneath.

The Kingdom of the Ill
(with apologies to S. Sontag)

You don't need a passport, not even a metaphorical one,
Nor is it dingy or cramped—it's vast,
Vast as Montana, with a population of one.
To get there you spend days, nights, shivering in the bed
Of a dreamy ex-ex-ex-lover's pick-up you don't remember
Getting in or out of. The last human voice you hear
Is Patsy Cline's moaning *As the skies turn gloomy/Night winds*
whisper to me...Wherever you lived now you live in a trailer;
You climb in through a busted window. There's a single scimitar
Of glass on the floor, a six-foot stack of your high school
Yearbooks. One spork, one glass, one can
Of Sweet Sue Chicken and Dumplings;
One vial of Roxonol 20 mg, one pile of rat shit.
There will be a forest of ten thousand trees
That are all the same tree, a cloud, a bird.
Beyond the river the roar of bulldozers, constantly.
Hours spent in psephomancy, xylomancy,
fashioning a purse of hair.
Minutes that float by like drowned ants.
With a screwdriver-tip red hot from the flame
Of your dead father's Zippo
You'll trace over your heart the silhouette of a church-bell.
Your dead father *who is beautiful like Quang Duc*
Setting himself aflame
You'll announce to the night-nurse, vaporous with morphine.
Long nights of driving a young-Tiger five iron though every living
Friend's head you can remember.
Of considering the known unknown.
It's not meant to be a revelation
When you discover the visitor before you has scrawled with red
Lipstick in spidery letters on the bathroom mirror
The shadow of the Great Pyramid of Cheops
And my shadow are the same age
With many exclamation marks.

Ullage

Odd word, for many a complete blank, but for him — annoying
At first, vexingly on the tip of the tongue, then a torment.
A feudal tax, a gully, something to do with the throat?
All day it taunts him. In the elevator, wandering to a meeting —
He's forgotten his phone, too. Finally
At lunchtime while he's waiting for a haircut
He thinks he has it, a dugout canoe
Hovers over the barber's head, then disappears.
How hateful these hours are! Stupid, stupid.
Isn't that what Sister Angela jeered? And, really,
Haven't we all felt it, trembling
As we stand beside our desk while she taps her black shoe?
All the other kids slack-jawed, staring, a hole opening up
Where our pride and anger leaks out, a sort of ullage,
The empty space left in a vessel measuring what's lacked.

Sonnet for Tony

After you'd passed, which I'd only just read about the next day on
    my cell
Up to my short-stay intern ears as I was in student forays
Into the strange world of contemporary Faronese poets
In rainy Prague, and now in the drab Žabka by my Airbnb
Rummaging for a pen through the new international everywhere
Cornucopia of SIM cards, Carmex, plastic pouches of kimchi,
While consequently feeling if I'm honest a little homesick,
A little meh, and yes very low, can I say I was more than glad
To suddenly hear another American voice in my ear?
Your sly smart beautiful utterly decent American
Voice, Tony, as you imparted what I've come to think
Of as your half-joking half-hopeful parting words to me Sharpied
On a dun-colored card propped before a dusty pyramid
Of Fun-Size Cherrios: *Vypršela - Stále Sobrá*! Expired – Still Good!

— for Tony Hoagland

The Mask

No more than a ragged head trimmed from a pillowcase found
At the dump after Halloween. So long ago now, I can still see

The loose threads turned black that dangled from its throat,
Cigarette holes for eyes, and for good cheer a crooked line

Of reddish lipstick suggesting a mouth I traced with my finger.
Held to the wind, it shivered. So long ago, but even at ten

I could see how he must have hated them.
The thankless chores, his cold room. The ghosts

Who made the ghost he must've been wear it.

Rose
— for M.L.

Lunaticus. Sub-order *Dermaptera*. A rare species of North American beetle with an attractive, pearl-ish exoskeleton and well-formed tarsus, this relative of the common earwig is best known, as its name implies, thanks to its strange behavior: after an unremarkable pubescence, and likely under the influence of an as yet undentifed neuroligical toxin, it abruptly returns to its former home in the alluvial substrate, where it promtly devolves into a sort of madness —incessantly folding and unfolding its sclerotized elytra while striking out aimlessly at perceived predators with a pair of vestigial pincers, for example, or with its iridescent forewings emitting a series of percussive clicks, as if repeatedly shutting and re-shutting a door. Although it should be noted these spasms, or "spells", are intermittent, and grow less pronounced with age. In fact, the few who have encountered this sad insect generally describe a creature so docile it appears almost paralyzed and can be easily stroked with a finger, even like a boutonniere affixed to a lapel — all the better, they say, to inhale its pungent but hardly unpleasant scent, like that of strong coffee, or the crumbling bindings of old books.

Also the beautiful speculative constellations of certain Medieval astronomers— the Officina Typographica, the Flying Squirrel— peremptorily consigned to oblivion by the Revised Harvard Photometry Catalog, like the saints Christopher, Ursula, and George

and the marble bust of child's head hovering in the velvet curtains of Ingres' "Portrait of Jaques Marquet De Montbreton De Norvins."

Perhaps the Finalandese word *leiko*: the phosphorescent blossoming of a tree trunk at the bottom of a mountain lake

Or *streichefrieden*, the act of gently stoking a dying animal.

A cobwebbed old gardener's shack like the first stirrings of a trumpet…

… ghost bike…bricked-up stained glass window…

the rose which only words far from roses can describe
wrote the great French poet Aragon.
And how else should I speak of you, dearest sister,
on this your death day?

The Arts of Love

Afraid I'd fall asleep to the late-afternoon lullaby
Of fenceposts and Swap Shop AM out past the last tree
And the Last Chance, I pulled over: a man in overalls.
Standing before pushed-together card tables
Laid with a crisp white sheet,
Where he'd positioned rows of antique tools—
Oiled up, exotic, fierce-looking things.
I recognized an auger, screwdrivers,
A grey-headed hammer, *ballpeen*.

The rest a mystery, but I was hooked, asking
This? and this? as I picked up a pair
Of red-lipped swiveled tongs that bit my finger,
Some sort of double-basined funnel,
A triangular brush sprung with stiff whiskers
Smelling of sour milk "For the Gotlands,"
— whatever that meant. Sweetheart,

it's true, I admit, I do often still see everything
Through the prism of sex. *Christ,
Even tools*…I could almost hear you thinking,
As I told you the story as finally back home in Tampa
With the French doors opened wide
To the humid evening you slipped out of your faded tee
And Mom jeans and put on those black panties
And Betty Paige bra I love… imagining
How in a few minutes I'd make Brandy Alexanders
And ferry them on a tray to our bed
Where you'd positioned yourself, glistening
And, yes, deliciously forbidding before me. The only question
Remaining whether this time you'd prefer
I play the old farmer who knew,
Or me in all my avid unknowing again.

Scraps

Chesterfields, buttercups in a bedside vase,
The cock of a cap on Sunday walks. Et cetera. Funny
How how the dead live on
These scraps of memory we feed them like dogs.
Always hungry, come-calling us by their name.

Pigeon-Toe

We found you in our neighbor's old garage.
For a week we took turns
Stroking your oily feathers, feeding you Dixie Loaf,
Popcorn, whatever. Then our pity wore out.

At the show, I was the emcee.
And now The Great Pigeon-Toe!
I announced to no one, as Billy took a rake handle
And beat on the rafters so you'd jump from one
To the other.

In the middle of the performance—
He must've swung a little too fast— you landed
With a thud and flapped crazily around in the cinders.
That was pretty funny. Then we went to baseball practice.

What did Balzac say— "Who is to decide which is
The grimmer sight: withered hearts, or empty skulls?"

In S—

I saw a man nearly cut in two by a car, he might've been taking a bow. Then he went swimming fully clothed over some train tracks, except for one shoe that landed in an ice-puddle; a teenager scooped it up, slipped one hand then the other inside. She was in diapers, covered in filth. When she smiled and raised the shoe beside her cheek, she looked like an animal I'd never seen before, with an enormous black ear and three teeth. I remember she wasn't shivering, the red lights of the ambulance. Twenty years I lived in that god-damned city, where is she now?

Poems from the Polio Ward [from Photographs and Captions from the Polio Ward, 1943-47
the Courier-Journal, Louisville, Kentucky]

"Dora S —, 8, Home Unit Iron Lung"

Among the experimental first, according to the article
"an unwieldy apparatus that fills half the living room" —although
one her parents have assured her is temporary: "like a cast
on a broken bone." A comparison, for now, she still finds
believable, as the accompanying photograph suggests: encased
in this humid armature, body thin as a wrist,
her gaze nevertheless serene, expectant; arrayed randomly
on its curved, off-white surface, these playful signatures —
— Eduardo!!!, MITCH, Sandy-Fay
swirled in girlish cursive—
not yet its implacable, un-scratchable itch.

"Phyllis Pleasant, 14, A "Sweet" Surprise"

Like her candy-striped pinafore and jaunty cap, her surname
an illusion her sullen smile belies: this "impromptu stand-in
for an unnamed MD called to an emergency surgery"
paused momentarily before a row of iron lungs. Puddled
at her feet, the sulphureous canvas bag
stenciled SOILED DIAPERS; a ragged red sweater
clasps her craned neck. Still, as instructed, she inventories
each item meticulously, in cramped cursive, on what appears
to be a scrolled length of teletype: sewing kit, cap gun,
a display case to be filled with scavenged rocks:
childish pleasures she must pretend aren't impossible yet,
as they must pretend she is Santa Claus.

Anonymous Girl, Aged 17, "Cured" Awaits Her Departure from St. Anthony's Hospital

Stiff-legged, ashen, emaciated— still, posed
against this mottled wall in her best black shoes
and frilly lace dress, cheeks freshly rouged, she peers
brightly into the camera as if startled
by a miraculous future— although one might also be forgiven
for thinking she's been newly dead for a century.
That, as memento mori, the burly photographer
has wrestled heavy wood slats under chemise and ruffled
sleeves to brace slack muscles; daubed that astonished gaze
on closed eyes. Also — a late arrival — a manicured hand
ferrying something reddish leftward into the frame— a rose,
perhaps, from the impossibly handsome doctor;
how, slightly blurred, she appears just about to turn
to thank him, and was speechless.

"Tommy S—, 11, Local Socialite's Son, After His First 'Field Trip' to Bardstown, Kentucky"

reads the caption beneath his picture: a frail, timid-looking boy,
posed in the hospital parking lot, eyes half-closed
but dutifully holding up a ticket and Official Songbook—
although of The Stephen Foster Story at the Wilderness Theater
one imagines he already remembers almost nothing:
not the long drive in the hired car, or the pair of muscled
of muscled attendants elbowing his wheelchair,
through the crowd; not "Sewanee River"
or all the silly dresses and buttoned, high-waisted trousers.
Only —perhaps with this slight smile— the little brown dog
that scampered on cue to the fastidious Matron's hand
then right off-stage toward the vast surrounding forest,
trailing its jeweled leash and blue bow, the tinkling of its polished
silver collar-bell that still could be heard, far off in the night.

"Nurse S —, the Florence Nightingale of the Polio Ward"

or perhaps that aging monster she wanly resembles —Roald Dahl's
Headmistress Trunchbull, drained of all wrath,
all resentment. Prim in her starched cap
and corseted frock, notebook in hand she has paused
at a boy's half-asleep head as if to record in meticulous particular
breaches of bedtime etiquette: appearance of tertiary paralysis,
evidence of paresthesia. Like her analog's,
vigilance now her lone, demented virtue, her thin smile
its ghastly exemplar: turned hastily toward the camera
as, departing, she draws this cozy pink coverlet
over his iron lung, a simulacrum of devotion.

Aster

A skinny dog puzzled by the shadow of its own tail,
someone who looks lost at a train station holding up a ticket,
a rusted playground rocket ship—
like so many things then like so many images of *after*
as I shuffled through a shoebox of old photographs
in those last days before the last hospital,
while watching you dead on your knees
but determined to ready the garden for winter.
The hose, stiffened, a lone circling hawk— maybe those, too.
And the tiny white aster, M—,
you'd plucked from a tangle of thornweed
and held up to show me; how once as I reached out
as if I could touch it, the fine film of sepia dust left by my fingertip
on the cold windowpane between us.

Sleek Green Car

The usual: vitals, follow-up labs, grainy screenshots
of my aching back —until, suddenly, "cancer"
                                    and like that!
the doctor disappeared,
taking with her 500 miles and almost sixty years.

Again, summer, Louisville, our clapboard house on Roland Street.
The screen door ajar, the stifled cry
of our new kitten Tim-Tam
crushed beneath the wheels… it was like I'd been split in two.
I, trembling, dazed …and—for a moment—I
the pony-tailed young girl singing along to the radio
in a sleek green car,
who didn't see, who never heard.

I Tell You This Now

In 1977, when the tornado as hunger blows through bodies blew
Through the nearby cemetery leaving only the chattering teeth
Of old wood gravestones and the naked carotene trunks
Of toppled elms, when it snatched
Up the adjacent Carmelite cloister and shook it, impaling
Two young postulants on shards of exploding rafters
As they huddled in the chapel,
Before heading further east to untangle two newlyweds
And wreathe their infant son in barbed wire,
I was alone in a quiet basement library room in a college reading
Robert Bly's *Silence in the Snowy Fields*.

I tell you this now, Tom, because you are dead. Because speaking
To the flawed dead who are perfect now is easy,
As I lean again tonight
Over your body, and stare a long time into your eyes
As through a train window veiled with soft dust, until the words
I read then but never got a chance to say come to me
As a few simple wishes: that despite the anguish and crazy hungers
That spiraled through your life, you too might have known
The calm I knew that afternoon of iron
Mailbox handles and dark tire tracks in snow, and somehow
Understood the salvation
Of Guinea hens hidden from the hired girl's hatchet
In impossible paces, asleep in the trees, even if that salvation was
Not yours; that if you trembled in your hospitable bed it was only
The slight trembling of words on white pages opened on a table,
Like the trembling of grass or water deep in the wells,
That is temporary; a wish that says, after the terrible whirlwind
Blew through it was as if on a train the conductor
Had poked you and you arrived out of the darkness
Suddenly awake to a strange new city, utterly happy.

Poem Against the Rich

It was late when I saw them, under a row of streetlamps
on a wide boulevard now deserted. Tall and slim,
one lingered outside a chic café,
while others stood before the windows
of galleries and cartographers' shops
or beneath a high feathered cap
galloped a magnificent steed through the alleyway.
It is good now to think of the dead, of the shadows
of courtesans, painters, explorers and brave sportsmen
passing unmolested through the iron bars of cemeteries
topped with sharp fletches dipped in gold
in the style of Louis IX, King of France,
also called *le Saint*, who among others of his lineage
lies in a lightless crypt in the *Basilique de Saint Denis*
below his sculpture badly carved in marble,
clutching his rosary, his fearsome sword
at his side, with its hilt encrusted in stolen rubies,
and his embroidered velvet slippers
that never once touched the earth.

Revelation on Pearson Avenue

Eating alone in the strange city, in an almost empty Chinese restaurant, still in his black suit
after the funeral and the wake, from the only other occupied table a man hears a tiny little crack,
then another man, about his age, also alone, but drunk, reading way too loud from his fortune cookie—

Would you rather drown in a sea of ignorance, or a sea of knowledge?

Not a glance from the bartender, the bored waiter. The first man, though, a little embarrassed,
looks out the window: across the street he sees a little guy shoving a woman wearing one shoe,
then down a little bit in a vacant lot, a big guy with a flashlight, bent over a metal detector.
Terrible, the diner thinks for a second …sad…or maybe not…Anyway, he's hungry, starts in on
his beef lo mein again.

Just then, as the story goes, behind one of those rice paper screens across the room, the diner hears a
second voice — you can't put your finger on it, but you know they're talking on a phone—

Well, as far as fathers go, that's pretty much the whole story, right?

Home Visit

In the kitchen, it's chaos again. Your brother the year-ago
   diagnosed schizophrenic
is shouting *Hey Boy*! and—really—*Satan*! into his untouched
   favorite home-visit
dinner of Rice-A Roni and Kool-Aid. He's fifteen, emaciated, still
   in his name-tagged whites
from Central State Hospital, with two black eyes and the
fragmented story of a blonde girl
drowned by someone named Tommy in the brackish retention
   pond there, a story interspersed
randomly with unearthly modulations of the word *gusto* as in
   Schlitz. It's 1966. The year before
he was Kentucky State Chess Champion, a theology prodigy
   bound for Princeton;
now he mimes masturbation standing before the living room
   mirror, carries in his back pockets
two paperbacks at all times: Thomas à Kempis's *Imitation of
   Christ*,
from which he can scythe verbatim great swathes of "Directives
   for the Interior Life,"
and Conrad Aiken's Collected Stories, whose short strange tale
"Silent Snow, Secret Snow" about a young boy's descent into
   madness he'll sing-song
lines from again tonight in his bare room. In other words, he's
   quite aware
of what's happening to him you've overheard your mother say to
   her friend Katsy
in a voice alchemically compounded of pride and shame, of pity
   and horror.
All of this and more, of course, you'll only piece together much
   later—
the Haldol, the Prolixin, the fifty-six mind-blowing sessions of
   ECT;
the 3 AM underpants wanderings, the squandering of whatever
   money he comes by
on drawing paper and acrylics that totter untouched in alpine
   stacks by his bed; the strangers
in ratty rabbit-fur coats and tank tops with no teeth or rotten teeth,

others incoherent,
flailing, one with his head staved in thanks to a motorcycle accident; strangers
from who knows where he'll invite home for silent hot-faced Sunday dinners
after church; not to mention his hand-scissored hair and chewed-off bleeding nails,
and the twitching and drooling of ropy belt-high strands of spittle due to early onset tardive
dyskinesia. OK. But for now you're ten. You have your baseball team, your new Stingray
with a banana seat and Mattel V-rroom! Real Motor Roar! Ten and half-asleep but listening
on the dark stairs, the sounds in the kitchen near but far, recast somehow in your boy-mind
as the scary old Icelandic lullaby your sailed-the-seven-seas Uncle Buck sings
so sweetly off-key when he's drunk:

Beeum, beeum, bambalow, Bambalow and dillidillidow.
My little friend I lull to rest.
But outside
A face looms at the window.

Or does that piece come later, too? Perhaps. Still, call it ten. You with your baseball
and bike feeling sleepily in your strange toy- heart there on the stairs a chill fear
that sinks its chill fingers in, a chaos that does not involve you yet but calls if not *Satan*!
Hey, Boy! to every trembling part of you.

1.8. 20—

Can I tell you, Father, at last,
after finding myself porn-blind and change jar
at the Bigfork Dollar Tree
and by last I mean ghost-delivered to my head this very minute
Blizzard'd-in twelve-pack Coors Light as I am
from the glacial, mind-scrubbing 5:45 P.M.
along with a few of my fellow desperados also wobbly in their
greasy snow duds that make us look like a pack
of janky Garcia Lorca's as we nudge our battered souls
from Magazines to Laundry to Salty Snacks
— can I tell you at last, Father, that I loved you?
That despite your every day ancient Anzio/wheelchair/VA rage
and nightly disappearing act,
spat fags, poetry, etc. also lately I hear MAGAA
up here in Montana I've just begun to seriously drunk-cry
and my friend Barry the manager
has laid his hand on my shoulder,
but my mind is still ten miles back on the iced-up interstate
where there's a new billboard going up southbound just past the
Arby's, featuring so far from what I could tell
a smiling little dog in a checkered overcoat and black fedora
with two legs blown off by the gale force wind,
the whole thing ghost-delivered to my heart that very minute
flickering on-off on-off in our slowly passing headlights
as if—can I tell you at last, Father,
since I saw you once from the neighbor's front porch—just as if
some determined old Fuller Brush man were approaching,
squiching through the swirling snow,
the windows of this house then that glowing now bright,
now quickly dark?

The Golden Frog

Named, of course, for the tale of the poison dart
That passes through one also to slay another—or in some cases
And another and another, until finally… pfftt. Newton's First Law.
According to my uncle, five was the Vietnam record in '66.
He'd seen it with his own eyes, the VC just lined 'em up
When they were short on bullets, he said, and for a moment
After we'd argued again today— the money, the women, the
    money, the kids—
I imagined my own life a little like this, D—,
How finally spent after all that as we stood together in the foyer
You pressed your finger lightly to my heart.

Crazy Lady

We'd called her; every neighborhood had one.
Ours grew cabbage and drove a three-wheeled car,
A *Messerschmitt*. It didn't take much.
Nazi! we'd scream and give her the Heil Hitler.
Late on summer nights we clattered her windows with crabapples,
Once we shot her little wiener dog Otto
Full of BB's, paralyzing him and shattering one eye;
I remember tossing him by the tail back and forth.
So many years ago, such cruelty, what can I say? We were ten,
We all have a little *Braunhemden* inside us,
A BB pistol or a crabapple or two stashed in a pocket?

Perhaps.

And now to the crazy lady.
Dear Reader, you know what I'm going to say:
We all have little bit of her inside, too.
Maybe half-forgotten, so small there trembling on the playground
In the wrong shoes, maybe the wrong color,
Can't figure out the cash register.
Maybe revved up one morning revving circles
In the neighbor's front yard, all the neighbors watching,
Before finally some little girl's father calls the cops,
Who come crashing through the cabbage
Past the Messerschmitt parked practically sideways in the carport
To find you, somebody says, still thrashing hanging
From a rafter in the shed.

Whoopee!

Cheap champagne of a word, a little musty
now, like "hurray" or "gosh" on the lips of haughty Susan Vance.
As an adjective, a kind of brimless crenelated cap
I remember our pious Galwegian da doffed before Sunday Mass;
also, as an almost-homonymic, the start of my little sister's
bad cough. Although strictly speaking "an exclamation
expressing wild excitement or joy" according to the OED, in
practice "widely considered as mocking, or used in irony:"
Whoopee! beneath my pen tonight
a chaste curse in the back when our old Ford took a sharp turn;
Whoopee! wheezed as she gripped the rails of her hospital cot
up the bright stairs, down the dark hall.

Ear Plugs
—from Lares and Penates

The size of three stacked nickels, made of pliable whitish-ish
 plastic, sticky—
old-fashioned candies, not very sweet.
For a good night's sleep, you have to press them in firmly
with both thumbs: imagine you're gouging out the eyes
of a harpie, or affixing a royal seal to a letter.
Even so, in the morning, sometimes one or the other, or both,
will have escaped, only to be found like a blob of ambergris
bobbing in the placid sea of one's blankets:
oily, slightly gray, covered with a dirty fuzz— disgusting! Still, isn't
it also a curious pleasure we feel, to hold this odd present
from the ear momentarily in the palm—overboiled duck's egg,
gelatinous rune, tiny brain of a shrunken head?
Before, enclosed in one fist and stretching the arms skyward,
rising somewhat groggily
to deposit it casually in the nearest bathroom wastebasket.

Why Write?

What if I told you once there was a father who chiseled
six live kittens out of his little son's cat's belly
with a drywall knife and smeared the slime and viscera
on the son's face, and dragged him from a shed behind him
along a trail through a field with one arm,
the other holding the faintly mewling kittens in a plastic bag,
before finally they arrived at a river where the father smashed the
bag against a shard of discarded granite
until the bag turned the color of cream and rust
and the mewling stopped, and he pitched it in the water?
Would you wonder if it was true, if I was that boy,
the terror of those minutes
blossoming momentarily in your mind like the awful flower the bag
resembled as it floated on the surface of the water?
And furthermore then
what if I also explained how a couple of eyeballs had fallen
out of the bag and the drunk father said
they looked like jellybeans,
and smeared with slime and viscera, demanded the boy eat one?
That for days he tasted it, the smell wouldn't wash off,
while in the shed its mother's carcass stayed covered in flies,
that if I could carve a poem out of this
I could do anything?

Prayer
for J—

Lord, let this girl live again.
Not in poems when they hatch, as they must, not suddenly
in some passing snatch of Titanic Mendelssohn
or hand me down old Elton John song
or ten thousand photographs, not as a vision
made all of mist and distant loon-calls hovering for an instant
on the shore of a certain forbidding Canadian lake where I've gone
alone to fish, not in a confused dream one night either,
just before I wake with the shakes
after I've sunk twelve shots of Patrón and swallowed
three of my nephew's Adderall—I've seen that face before
and it isn't hers.
Lord, no – let this girl live again.
She who never once knew the ocean or the pleasurable heft
of a good pen. The way the deft bishop darts
diagonally behind the rook. Is this too much to ask? I beg You.
Let her sulk and sob and chop off all her hair,
if it pleases You somehow.
Then if You can manage it, You who manage all things,
call a general school holiday, topple the cell towers,
make her rising before dawn
be merely to wander again as she loved to the safe
leafy streets of our neighborhood, and when she finally tires,
O, Lord, let her lie back gently in the cattails by the creek
in the park by our house
not with a gun in her hand but, say, a daisy, nice and pink,
rimmed with fresh dew, from her impossibly beautiful boyfriend.

In Basel

Gone, my sister finally breathes, *Gone*, looking up, when
Our stepmother dies in her arms, after the usual horrors.

…great pain, the long, slow pain that takes its time…
by which we are burned as with green wood…

Wrote Nietzsche, whose university rooms
 I can see from the window

When I get up to look for the ambulance.
Something like that. Though

It wasn't until later, long after they'd packed up the body
And handed us what amounted to a business card

That I suddenly remembered another, famous one:
Every word also a mask. E.g.,

The hopeful *more* we heard in *morte* each time
Her French flatmate spoke.

The way-worn *Go* in that woeful *Gone*.

When I Got the News

That you had finally killed yourself, M --,
I was standing in the hall

Outside my sixth grade Catechism class.
Father was vague.

One shoe was untied, his red tie askew.
I can still see them

Through the chicken-wired glass:
The solemn faces, my empty desk,

The word TRANSUBSTANTIATION
Freshly underlined on the blackboard,

Sister Angela's voluminous black sleeve
And a fine cloud of white dust

Drifting toward the open window.

Lonely Marriage
— from Fables of The Midwest

The wife is a professor, Contemporary Literature, Ohio State, stern, loves to be right. He was her best student, handsome, played guitar in a band, blah, blah, a long time ago. Anyway, they've argued, it doesn't matter: he knows the trick — an I.T. guy now, he isn't stupid. So the husband starts to recite aloud, from memory, one of his wife's favorite poems…

But it's late, pretty soon he can feel her pulling the duvet over her head. After a few minutes he lays his watch and his glasses on the bedstand, turns out the light, pecks her hair goodnight.

Morning comes. In an old jewelry box next to his cup of coffee, there's a little porcelain figurine smashed to bits, under a handwritten note —

an old tortoise
who's tame enough to ride
too huge to slaughter

In this version, the husband says to himself, Okay. They don't speak about it. Things go on.
In another version, there's just a cup of coffee.

The Uncanny

is an artist, but even for an artist a pretty weird and imperious one. Last week, for example, she sent her assistant out to gather up a lot of voles. Voles? her assistant asked. Voles, the Uncanny said. Where am I going to find voles in New York City, and what the fuck does she mean by a lot? the assistant wondered. Still, he checked out the pet shops, even found himself tramping around Pelham Bay. No voles. The Uncanny was pissed. Last week it was canceled stamps from Nagorno-Karabach and before that he'd stayed up all night yanking the mechanical voice boxes out of 48 Chatty Cathy heads. Fine, the Uncanny had said, good job, when the assistant staggered up the stairs with two big cardboard boxes. Seriously, though, what about the voles? And the prosthetic ear? Oh, and shadows, you can never have too many shadows…

Daniel

My name. Shared with many others,
Dead and living, a few famous, most not,
Yet with each of whom I feel an elusive but undeniable
Kinship; meaningless in my mouth
As it must be in the ears of my niece's pet rabbit,
Stale bread on the lips of others.
My twin, according to the Ancients;
For the Romantics, "the shadow
with whom a man travels all his days".
But is it I who look like you, or you like me?
And if you are like my constant shadow why
Then whenever we meet is it always as if for the first time,
Daniel, how is it even etched on this familiar park bench
On 77th Street set among overturned pink children's bikes
And wildflowers you somehow frighten me?

Dither

Strange word: a little feather in it, a little wooden top.
A darting tropical fish, or an Urdu diacritical mark.
The sound a small boy might make
Pointing to his infant sister. Often pejorative,
Suggesting an inappropriate lack of gravity
With regard to certain circumstances.
Picture Nero, a fire. My father in the next room
Wondering aloud whether he should wear
The black or the dark navy-blue socks to her funeral.

It was there

in everywhere cough pocketknife & rain-soaked gutter Playboy
rusty swing set & fag & colored in Sansabelt
& grimy fingerprint light switch in lipstick as in library & jimmied
St. Paul's poor box in the saccharine reek of Christmas
Hai Karate & Purina dogfood plant
in endless November December January February March
with slush & potted ham & 1000 x's Hi-Fi Andy Williams
Moon River plus Barbicide & old lady coin purse
in galoshes and the word *galoshes*
or as our pie-eyed ex- Galway Da waxing philosophic
would pronounce again to absolutely nobody as we'd bounce
ancient Nash Metropolitan homebound
from every infant's wife's or old fucker's wake I can remember
death is death we'll all find it soon enough
while jammed in the backseat M—& I
would roll our eyes & wish for it as if wasn't all around us already
everywhere we looked if we'd cared to look
in that God-damned county as if there were a dearth of it

Ars Poetica

Let come the lemon tree.
Not its skewbald bark or its blossoms' pianissimo perfume
replayed in the nostrils as one sultry summer's distillate,
not *very pretty* or its bunches of ragged leaves clenched like fists
at the breast of some ancient Persian queen; not where you kissed
Sam or Teisha, or, as symbol, half-peeled
in Willem Kalf's luminescent "Still Life with Chinese Bowl;"
not as madeleine, either—its faded emblem regarded on a rusted
can of Quist— or the fresh calligraphy of its shadowed twigs
on the old scarred desk.
But, merely, the lemon tree.
After ten thousand thousand books of poetry, this is the dream.

Childhood

Though childhood is not what a child would know
To call it—her corpus callosum isn't quite
Connected yet—and anyway why would she want to?
When you're six you're a ghost inside another ghost,
Un-pierceable by anything in the substantial world,
Where this and this and this keeps happening.
A knob of milky quartz juts out of a rock.
There's a man on the moon, a box of matches adorned with a key.
You wear your life lightly
As the dog you name wears the name you name it.

ABOUT THE AUTHOR

Daniel Lawless is the author most recently of *The Gun My Sister Killed Herself With*. Recent poems appear in *FIELD*, *Barrow Street*, *Prairie Schooner*, *Ploughshares*, *Poetry International*, Los Angeles Review, *upsteet*, *SOLSTICE*, *Manhattan Review*, *Massachusetts Review*, *JAMA*, and *Dreaming Awake: New Prose Poetry from the U.S., Australia,* and the U.K., among others. A recipient of a continuing Shifting Foundation grant, he is the founder and editor of *Plume: A Journal of Contemporary Poetry*, *Plume Editions*, and the annual *Plume Poetry anthologies*.

Printed in the USA
CPSIA information can be obtained
at www.ICGtesting.com
LVHW091403200724
785991LV00003B/622